Quote Unquote III

A Student's Lesson

Kenya Dryden

ISBN 978-1-09830-941-1 eBook 978-1-09830-942-8

"I see my path, but I don't know where it leads. Not knowing where I'm going is what inspires me to travel it."

Rosalia de Castro

"Man ought to believe that he is capable of accomplishing anything that he places his mind upon."

Kenya K. Dryden

"Life takes us to unexpected places
I don't know where I am going but I am on my way."

Carl Sagan

"When you look for the good in everything,
somehow you will always be led to find it."

Kenya K. Dryden

"If you asked me for my New Year resolution,
it would be to find out who I am"

Cyril Cusack

"Be active in opportunity"

Kenya K. Dryden

"I think in terms of the day's resolutions, not the years."

Henry Moore

"The success of anything can only be reached by
going beyond one's own confidence."

Kenya K. Dryden

"Although no one can go back and make a brand-
new start, anyone can start from now and make
a brand-new ending."

Carl Bard

"Medicate your mind with principles."

Kenya K. Dryden

"No Matter how hard the past, you can always begin again."

Buddha

"Every day will not be filled with cheerfulness, but every day that is lived should be cheered."

Kenya K. Dryden

"Always bear in mind that your own resolution to succeed is more important than any other."

Abraham Lincoln

"Seek nothing for yourself that you would
not equally help another seek for
himself or herself."

Kenya K. Dryden

"Be structured enough for success and achievement,
and flexible enough for creativity and fun."

Taylor Duvall

"Be mindful that every powerful and subtle
influence of the mind can externalize
long before it is necessary.

Kenya K. Dryden

"Success is not final, failure is not fatal: it is the courage to continue that counts."

Winston Churchhill

"A wise man knows that his ways should never be directed in selfishness."

Kenya K. Dryden

"You must do the things you think you cannot do."

Eleanor Roosevelt

"Above all things, become someone who consistently learns."

Kenya K. Dryden

"Ever Tried. Ever Failed. No Matter. Try Again. Fail Again. Fail Better."

Samuel Beckett

"Always find a way to measure your approach
in responding to diverse characters."

Kenya K. Dryden

"I will not try to convince you to love me, to respect
me, to commit to me. I deserve better than
that; I AM BETTER THAN THAT...Goodbye."

Steve Maraboli

"Love can only reign supreme when you allow it to grow."

Kenya K. Dryden

"If you don't know where you want to go, then it
doesn't matter which path you take."

Alice in Wonderland

"Fear and worry are two of the most expensive mental states to entertain. You pay more into these two things only to gain, nothing."

Kenya K. Dryden

"There are far, far better things ahead than any we leave behind."

C. S. Lewis

"An inherited past is meant to be transformed into a better future."

Kenya K. Dryden

"You are never too old to re-invent yourself."

Steve Harvey

"We must learn to do, before we can teach what
must be done and most of all we must
learn to live before we can speak about living."

Kenya K. Dryden

"If you can't fly, then run.
If you can't run, then walk.
If you can't walk, then crawl.
But whatever you do, you have to keep moving forward."

Martin Luther King, Jr.

"It is through the mind that the body becomes rich, becomes healthy and becomes strong."

Kenya K. Dryden

"Don't wait for the perfect moment.
Take the moment and make it perfect."

Zoey Sayward

"Any scholar who has ripened through his lessons
and is considered a venerated teacher
must be an exponent of noble character. This shall
be, so that he can reflect what still lives
and what will continue to exist."

Kenya K. Dryden

"That a man can change himself and master his own
destiny is the conclusion of every mind who
is wide-awake to the power of right thought."

Christian D. Larson

"Fear not the challenges before you; for they are
the doorway to endless possibilities."

Kenya Dryden

"The unexamined life is not worth living."

Socrates

"Imprint the very essence of hope in your mind and
out of your heart will spring the desire's
hoped for."

Kenya Dryden

"Knowing yourself is the beginning of all WISDOM."

Aristotle

"Truth knows no error; it is greater than the
existence of any creed and it runs deeper
than every known dogma to man.

Kenya K. Dryden

"Knowing others is intelligence;
Knowing yourself is true wisdom;
Mastering others is strength;
Mastering yourself is true power."

Lao Tzu

"Be prudent enough to give thought to your
ways and you will not be led to simply
believe anything."

Kenya Dryden

"Any fool can know. The point is to understand."

Albert Einstein

"Cause and effect does not produce chance, it produces facts."

Kenya Dryden

"Here's to the crazy ones. The misfits. The rebels.
The troublemakers. The round pegs in the
square holes. The ones who see things differently.
They're not fond of rules. And they have no
respect for the status quo. You can quote them,
disagree with them, glorify or vilify them.
About the only thing you can't do is ignore them.
Because they change things. They push the
human race forward. And while some may see them
as the crazy ones, we see genius.Because
the people who are crazy enough to think they can
change the world, are the ones who do."

Rob Siltanen

"Common sense is the supreme regulator of
life. It is meant to be used often."

Kenya Dryden

"Twenty years from now you will be more disappointed
by the things that you didn't do than by
the ones you did do. So, throw off the bowlines.
Sail away from the safe harbor. Catch the
trade winds in your sails. Explore. Dream. Discover."

H. Jackson Brown, Jr.

"From the lips of a wise man, his words will rise with truth. From the lips of a fool, his words in pride shall fall."

Kenya Dryden

"People are illogical, unreasonable, and self-centered
Love them anyway.
If you do good, people will accuse you of selfish ulterior motives.
Do good anyway.
If you are successful, you will win false friends and true enemies.
ucceed anyway.
The good you do today will be forgotten tomorrow.
Do good anyway.
Honesty and frankness make you vulnerable.
Be honest and frank anyway.
The biggest men and women with the biggest ideas can be shot
down by the smallest men and women with the smallest minds.
Think big anyway.
People favor underdogs but follow only top dogs.
Fight for a few underdogs anyway.
What you spend years building may be destroyed overnight.
Build anyway.
eople really need help but may attack you if you do help them.
Help people anyway.
Give the world the best you have and you'll get kicked in the teeth.
Give the world the best you have anyway."

Keith M. Kent

"Any person who entertains the thoughts of hatred
will suffer far more than the one who
is being hated."

Kenya Dryden

"I must say a word about fear. It is life's only true opponent.
Only fear can defeat life. It is a clever, treacherous adversary,
how well I know. It has no decency, respects no law or
convention, shows no mercy. It goes for your weakest spot,
which it finds with unnerving ease. It begins in your mind, always...so
you must fight hard to express it. You must fight hard to shine the light
of words upon it. Because if you don't, if your fear becomes a wordless
darkness that you avoid, perhaps even manage to forget, you open
yourself to further attacks of fear because you never truly fought the
opponent who defeated you."

Yann Martel

"It is with words, of how they are expressed or written,
that simply conveys different opinions
to the mind."

Kenya Dryden

"Man is a mystery. It needs to be unraveled, and if you spend your whole life unravelling it, don't say that you've wasted time. I am studying that mystery because I want to be a human being."

Fyodor Dostoyevsky

"Judging someone before knowing them calls for a
modification, in the life of the one who is
doing the judging."

Kenya Dryden

"No! Try not. Do, or do not. There is no try."

George Lucas, The Star Wars Trilogy

"Leave no man bewildered. Lead him to authentic learning."

Kenya Dryden

"Maybe each human being lives in a unique world, a private
world different from those inhabited and experienced by all
other humans…If reality differs from person to person, can we
speak of reality singular, or shouldn't we really be talking about
plural realities? And if there are plural realities, are some more true
(more real) than others? What about the world of a schizophrenic?
maybe it's as real as our world. Maybe we cannot say that we are in
touch with reality and he is not, but should instead say, His reality is so
different from ours that he can't explain
his to us, and we can't explain ours to him. The
problem, then, is that if subjective worlds are
experienced too differently, there occurs a breakdown in
communication…and there is the real illness."

Philip K. Dick

"The best place to meet a person right where they are is in PRAYER."

Kenya Dryden

"If you understand others you are smart.
If you understand yourself, you are illuminated.
If you overcome others you are powerful.
If you overcome yourself, you have strength.
If you know how to be satisfied you are rich.
If you can act with vigor, you have a will.
If you don't lose your objectives, you can be long-lasting.
If you die without loss, you are eternal."

Lao Tzu, Tao Te Ching

"Let every created vision be fulfilled by the facts."

Kenya Dryden

"Your pain is the breaking of the shell that encloses your understanding…And could you keep your heart in wonder at the daily miracles of your life, your pain would not seem less wonderous than your joy."

Kahlil Gibran

"Man must represent and obey the realities that they create."

Kenya Dryden

"I don't want to be a tree; I want to be its meaning."

Orhan Pamuk, My Name is Red

"Mistakes are to be made, by the man and for
the man, for sound instruction."

Kenya Dryden

"Things do not change; we change."

Henry David Thoreau

"Never smother the nature of curiosity. It produces
the desire to seek new facts at a time
when they need to be found."

Kenya Dryden

"No one should ever ask themselves that: why am I unhappy?
The question carries within it the virus that will destroy
everything. If we ask that question, it means we want to find
out what makes us happy. If what makes us happy is different
from what we have now, then we must either change once and for all or
stay as we are, feeling even more unhappy."

Paul Coelho

"No man is certain of his observations, just practical in his impression of what is being observed.

Kenya Dryden

"The eyes sees only what the mind is prepared to comprehend."

Robertson Davies

"The only way to an everlasting victory is through training in truth."

Kenya Dryden

"What you are is God's gift to you, what you become is your gift to God."

Hans Urs von Balthasar, Prayer

"We attract what we consciously or unconsciously invite."

Kenya Dryden

"When another blames you or hates you, or people voice similar criticisms, go to their souls, penetrate inside and see what sort of people they are. You will realize that there is no need to be racked with anxiety that they should hold any particular opinion about you."

Marcus Aurelius, Meditations

"What has been done is a guideline for what needs to be done."

Kenya Dryden

"Wisdom cannot be imparted. Wisdom that a wise man attempts to impart always sounds like foolishness to someone else…Knowledge can be communicated, but not wisdom. One can find it, live it, do wonders through it, but one cannot communicate and teach it."

Hermann Hesse, Siddhartha

"When improving your mind, seek out the most
noblest instruments that can distinctively
Shape your ideas."

Kenya Dryden

"The surest way of concealing from others the boundaries of one's own knowledge is not to overstep them."

Giacomo Leopardi

"Always give thought to your ways and the discernment of knowledge will come easily."

Kenya Dryden

"Unless you try to do something beyond what you have already
mastered, you will never grow."

Ronald E. Osborn

"Any man can be an advocate of destruction when
he has not learned how to creatively build."

Kenya Dryden

"An investment in knowledge always pays the best interest."

Benjamin Franklin, The Way to Wealth: Ben Franklin on Money and Success

"Your identity is not who you are on the outside,
it's who you are on the inside."

Kenya Dryden

"Remember my friend, that knowledge is stronger than memory, and we should not trust the weaker."

Bram Stoker

"When you labor in the spirit of good will toward
the nature of all men, nothing is to
be gained but light and the dignity of its truth."

Kenya Dryden

"What transforms this world is – knowledge. Do you see what I mean? Nothing else can change anything in this world. Knowledge alone is capable of transforming the world, while at the same time leaving it exactly as it is. When you look at the world with knowledge, you realize that things are unchangeable and at the same time are constantly being transformed."

Yukio Mishima

"When you can create order in your current
state, there you will find happiness and
all things better."

Kenya Dryden

"Do not think of knocking out another person's brains because he differs in opinion from you. It would be as rational to knock yourself on the head because you differ from yourself ten years ago."

Horace Mann

"What have been done is a guideline to what needs to be done."

Kenya Dryden

"Any fool can know. The point is to understand."

Albert Einstein

"To be great, learn how to use a level of observation
and imagination that will verifythe vision."

Kenya Dryden

"Dare to Be

When a new day begins, dare to smile gratefully.

When there is darkness, dare to be the first to shine a light.

When there is injustice, dare to be the first to condemn it.

When something seems difficult, dare to do it anyway.

When life seems to beat you down, dare to fight back.

When there seems to be no hope, dare to find some.

When you're feeling tired, dare to keep going.

When times are tough, dare to be tougher.

When love hurts you, dare to love again.

When someone is hurting, dare to help them heal.

When another is lost, dare to help them find a way.

When a friend falls, dare to be the first to extend a hand.

When you cross paths with another, dare to make them smile.

When you feel great, dare to help someone else feel great too.

When the day has ended, dare to feel as you've done your best.

Dare to be the best you can –

At all times, Dare to be!"

Steve Maraboli

"There are no truces without peace in the spirit of reconciliation."

Kenya Dryden

"Failure is the condiment that gives success its flavor."

Truman Capote

"The mind does not know any better than the man who is lost."

Kenya Dryden

"Letting go means to come to the realization that some people are a part of your history, but not a part of your destiny."

Steve Maraboli

"The deepest revelation to be understood in life is action."

Kenya Dryden

"How would your life be different if…You stopped making negative judgmental assumptions about people you encounter? Let today be the day…You look for the good in everyone you meet and respect their journey."

Steve Maraboli

"Condition your circumstances or become a condition of circumstance."

Kenya Dryden

"A thinker sees his own actions as experiments and questions- - as attempts to find out something. Success and failure are for him answers above all."

Friedrich Nietzsche

"Ultimately, it is the man that knows better, not the mind."

Kenya Dryden

"Success is not how high you have climbed, but how you make a positive difference to the world."

Roy T. Bennett

"Man can face his own ruin if he does not
have the patience to wait in faith."

Kenya Dryden

"Don't aim at success. The more you aim at it and make it a target, the more you are going to miss it. For success, like happiness, cannot be pursued; it must ensue, and it only does so as the unintended side effect of one's personal dedication to a cause greater than oneself or as the by-product of one's surrender to a person other than oneself. Happiness must happen, and the same holds for success: you have to let it happen by not caring about it. I want you to listen to what your conscience commands you to do and go on to carry it out to the best of your knowledge. Then you will live to see that in the long-run –in the long-run, I say! – success will follow you precisely because you had forgotten to think about it."

Viktor E. Frankl

"Many are attracted to the things that can only be seen."

Kenya Dryden

"Kites rise highest against the wind, not with it."

Winston S. Churchill

"Only a real sculpture can be identified in time and space with his chisel."

Kenya Dryden

"When you show yourself to the world and display your talents, you naturally stir all kinds of resentment, envy, and other manifestations of insecurity, you cannot spend your life worrying about the petty feelings of others."

Robert Greene

"The light of God rises on every man, as long as he has life."

Kenya Dryden

"Supreme excellence consists of breaking the enemy's
resistance without fighting."

Sun Tzu

"The heart is the source from which you believe. It would be wise to follow it and live a life that catches your heart on purpose."

Kenya Dryden

"Judge your success by what you had to give up in order to get it."

Dalai Lama XIV

"Failure is worth finding all of the ways that will not work."

Kenya Dryden

"The difference between a successful person and others is not a lack of strength, not a lack of knowledge, but rather a lack in will."

Vince Lombardi Jr.

"Do not allow your thinking to become futile
and your hearts to become darkened."

Kenya Dryden

"I've come to believe that each of us has a personal calling that's as unique as a fingerprint – and that the best way to succeed is to discover what you love and then find a way to offer it to others in the form of service, working hard, and also allowing the energy of the universe to lead you."

Oprah Winfrey

"Make it a daily practice to measure the limits
that you place on your knowledge."

Kenya Dryden

"In order to succeed, your desire for success should be greater than your fear of failure."

Bill Cosby

"It is from the root that a flower will take its shape
and grow. It must trust the process of growth
without seeing the root from which it grows."

Kenya Dryden

"…it is well known that a vital ingredient of success is not knowing that what you're attempting can't be done."

Terry Pratchett

"Everything that is certain to be understands
that nothing happens by chance,
it only happens by design."

Kenya Dryden

"The only way that we can live, is if we grow. The only way that
we can grow is if we change. The only way that we can change is
if we learn. The only way that we can become exposed is if we throw
ourselves out into the open. Do it. Throw yourself."

C. JoyBell C.

"It is a joyful thing when the ability to persevere
through trials of many kinds can
produce faith.

Kenya Dryden

"People tend to complicate their own lives, as if living weren't already complicated enough."

Carlos Ruiz Zafron

"In the space between thinking and feeling, you
will always find a reigning wisdom."

Kenya Dryden

"There will be a few times in your life when all your instincts
will tell you to do something, something that defies logic,
upsets your plans and may seem crazy to others. When that
happens, you do it. Listen to your instincts and ignore
everything else. Ignore logic, ignore the odds, ignore the complications,
and just go for it."

Judith McNaught

"The pursuit of happiness ends at a destination, but it
continues through the duration of a journey
that knows no end."

Kenya Dryden

"Give out what you most want to come back."

Robin S. Sharma

"Only those who are not strangers to the truth,
knows that truth imitates what is good."

Kenya Dryden

"Be a lamp, or a lifeboat, or a ladder. Help someone's soul heal.
Walk out of your house like a shepherd."

Jalaluddin Mevlana Rumi

"You cannot be wise in another man's learning.
You must seek to learn what makes you
wise on your own.

Kenya Dryden

"You were born to win, but to be a winner you must plan to win, prepare to win and expect to win."

Zig Ziglar

"When in doubt, dismiss the very things that insult
your soul and re-examine what has been
spoken.

Kenya Dryden

"Sometimes the only way to ever find yourself is to get completely lost."

Kellie Elmore

"Do not look back with the eyes for sorrow or look
around with the eyes for worry. Use the eyes
to look upward in Faith knowing that you have placed
your gaze in the best possible direction, as
you stand below.

Kenya Dryden

"Life consists of two days, one for you one against you. So, when it's for you don't be proud or reckless, and when it's against you be patient, for both days are a test for you."

Hazrat Ali Ibn Abu-Talib A.S.

"The tongue can cause a fire, or it can prevent a fire.
Let it be an instrument that quench souls
to extinguish the flames that they run toward.

Kenya Dryden

"In breaking away from the familiar and the expected, you'll be forced and privileged to face greater challenges, learn harder lessons, and really get to know yourself."

Kelly Cutrone

"It is best to use time wisely, as it is hard to imagine what it would mean to kill time without affecting eternity.

Kenya Dryden

"I like to believe that you don't need to reach a certain goal to be happy. I prefer to think that happiness is always there, and that when things don't go the way we might like them to, it's a sign from above that something even better is right around the corner."

David Archuleta

"Only those who are wise understand that they can
get more use from their enemies, than
a fool can get from the people that he or she consider to be friends."

Kenya Dryden

"People are successful because they think and act like successful people."

Roy T. Bennett

"The heart is the source from which you believe. It would be wise to follow it and live a life that catches your heart on purpose."

Kenya Dryden

"Don't complain, don't explain."

Raymond Carver

"Never speak words that you will regret,
when you can choose to be silent."

Kenya Dryden

"Life is an experiment in which you may fail or succeed. Explore more, expect least."

Santosh Kalwar

"The true nature of existence is to re-discover
and become the person that was
once lost, but now who is found.

Kenya Dryden

"The person may have a scar, but it also means they have a story."

Jodi Picoult

"The process of realization can accomplish more than the process of affirmation, although affirmation is considered an aid to realization.

Kenya Dryden

"The voice says, maybe you don't go to hell for the things you do. Maybe you go to hell for the things you don't do. The things you don't finish."

Chuck Palahniuk

"It is the mental attitude that corresponds with the cause to determine the extent of the effect.

Kenya Dryden

"To protect themselves, the weak focus on the "bad" in people. Conversely, the strong, who fear little, focus on the "good"."

Limani David

"Every elevation of life should be worn in
meekness and humility to bypass
any confusion of glorifying the self."

Kenya Dryden

"Don't ever live vicariously. This is your life. Live."

Lavinia Spalding